Practise Percentages

Contents

Introduction	2
Estimating percentages	3
Out of 100	5
Percentages, fractions and decimals	7
Calculating percentages in your head	9
Calculating other percentages	11
Calculating percentages with a calculator	13
Activity cards	15
Writing something as a percentage	19
Problems, problems	21
Estimating percentage increases and decreases	23
Percentage increases	25
Percentage decreases	27
Increasing and decreasing more than once	29
Answers	31

Introduction

Practise Percentages

Practise Percentages is for anyone who is struggling to understand concepts in percentages like calculating percentages of quantities and doing percentage increases and decreases, as well as all the other difficult ideas usually covered in maths lessons at Key Stage 3. Percentages is a topic that most people find difficult at first, but this simple, step-by-step approach should have you calculating percentages in your head and on a calculator in no time.

Part 1 of this book is all about understanding percentages, estimating and calculating them and converting them to fractions and decimals. Part 2 deals with percentage change, including finding percentage increases and decreases in real-life problems. Also covered is writing an amount as a percentage of another amount.

How to use *Practise*

Work through each section in order, reading all the clues and tips as you go through the exercises. You will need to cut out the cards in the centre of the book to use for some activities. Make sure you keep these cards in a safe place, such as an envelope, so you can re-use them.

When you feel confident with what is written on a particular page, turn over and try to answer the questions on the next page. Carefully mark all your answers and see how you got on. If you are still stuck and feel that you need some more practice, try some of the activities again or re-read the tips and comments in the margins. If you feel confident and have got most of the questions right, move on to the next section.

You might find it helpful to make a list of all the key words you come across in this book and write down the meanings. This will help you when you try to answer the questions.

First published in 2004
exclusively for WHSmith by
Hodder Murray, a member of the Hodder Headline Group
338 Euston Road
London NW1 3BH

Impression number   10 9 8 7 6 5 4 3 2 1
Year   2010 2009 2008 2007 2006 2005 2004

Text and illustrations © Hodder Murray 2004

All rights reserved. Apart from any use permitted under UK copyright law, no part of this publication may be reproduced or transmitted in any form or by any means, electronic or mechanical, including photocopying, recording, or any information storage and retrieval system, without permission in writing from the publisher or under licence from the Copyright Licensing Agency Limited. Further details of such licences (for reprographic reproduction) may be obtained from the Copyright Licensing Agency Limited, of 90 Tottenham Court Road, London W1T 4LP.

Text: Hilary Koll and Steve Mills (e-mail: info@cmeprojects.com)
Typeset by Fakenham Photosetting Limited, Fakenham, Norfolk

Printed and bound in Spain

A CIP record for this book is available from the British Library

ISBN 0 340 81329 6

Estimating percentages

Percentages tell us how much of a whole something is

Make a good guess

- Cut out all the percentage cards on page 15.

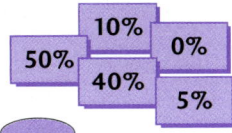

100% This card is *one hundred percent* and it means 'the whole'.

(100% of them were male.) (The shirt is 100% cotton.) (I scored 100% in a test.)

75% This card is *seventy-five percent* and it means 'three-quarters'.

(75% of them were male.) (The shirt is 75% cotton.) (I scored 75% in a test.)

50% This card is *fifty percent* and it means 'a half'.

(50% of them were male.) (The shirt is 50% cotton.) (I scored 50% in a test.)

25% This card is *twenty-five percent* and it means 'a quarter'.

(25% of them were male.) (The shirt is 25% cotton.) (I scored 25% in a test.)

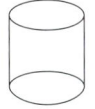

0% This card is *zero percent* and it means 'none' or 'nothing'.

(0% of them were male.) (The shirt is 0% cotton.) (I scored 0% in a test.)

Try it yourself! ▼

Estimate what percentage of each container is filled and find a card showing that percentage.

★ Estimating

Making an estimate is like having a good guess at something. It happens all the time in real life.

Imagine that a footballer has hurt his ankle. His manager might make an estimate as to how likely he is to play on Saturday. He might say, 'There's a 60% chance that he'll be better by then.'

★ Don't worry about estimating

People sometimes worry that their estimates will be wrong. It does not matter if the manager was not exactly right – it was just an estimate to give people some idea.

Do not worry, just practise saying roughly what percentage of each container in **Try it yourself!** is filled.

⭐ Clues and tips

When estimating, always keep percentages such as 75%, 50% and 25% in mind.

Think to yourself:

Is it more or less than a half, a quarter or three-quarters?

⭐ What next?

If you are fine with estimating percentages, go on to page 5. If not, cut out two different coloured circles from card. On each circle make a straight cut to the centre. Slide them together like this:

Twist them to create different percentages of a circle (as in question 2).

Now practise estimating what percentage of the circle is shaded.

Try it yourself!

1 By drawing lines, match each container with an appropriate estimate.

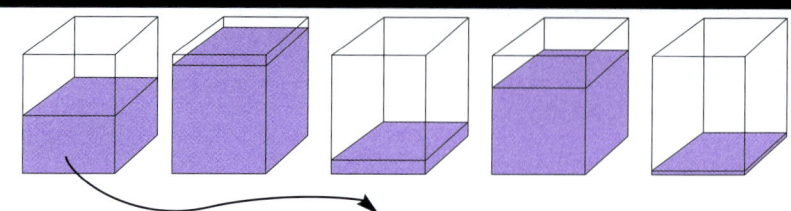

2 By drawing lines, match each shape with an appropriate estimate.

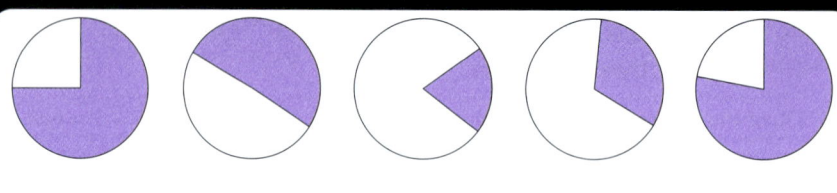

3 Estimate roughly what percentage of each shape is shaded.

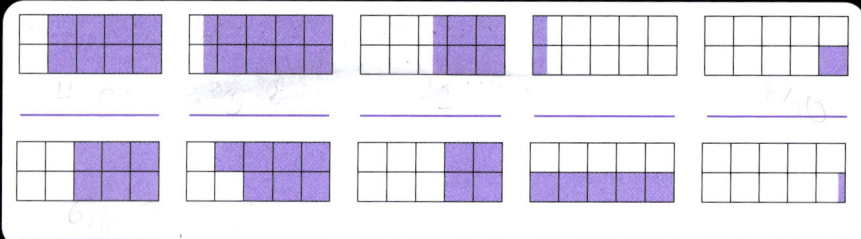

Have you got it?

Tick here

I understand that percentages tell us how much of a whole something is

I know that 50% is a half, 75% is three-quarters and 25% is a quarter

I can estimate percentages of shapes and containers

4

Out of 100

It's easier than estimating

- Instead of having to guess a percentage, it helps if the shape or container shows 100 equal parts.

 is 53 out of 100 equal parts

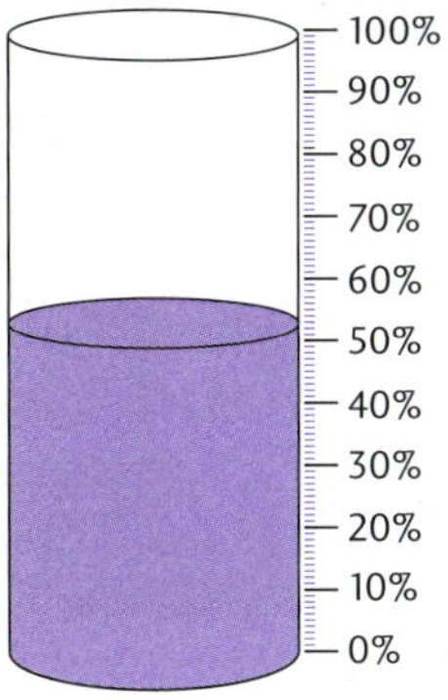

Each percentage can be written in three different ways. As a:

(percentage)   (fraction)   (division)

53%   or $\frac{53}{100}$ or   53 ÷ 100

- Some percentages can be written as fractions in *more than one* way. Write each of these as a fraction (out of 100).

| 50% | 10% | 25% | 75% | 20% |

$\frac{50}{100}$ ___   ___   ___   ___

- Notice that each fraction can be changed to its simplest form by dividing the top and bottom numbers by the same number. Change each fraction above to its simplest form by dividing.

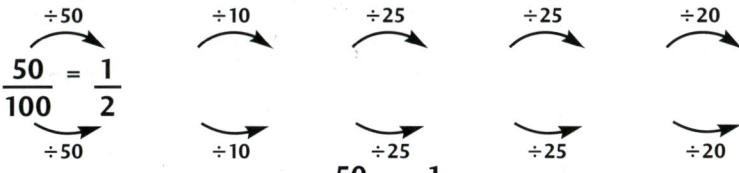

- So, 50% can be written as $\frac{50}{100}$ or $\frac{1}{2}$.

Try it yourself!

Pick a percentage card and describe it:

- as a fraction (out of 100)
- and as a division question (divided by 100).

Do this several times to get the hang of it.

Always think of the % sign as 'out of 100' or 'divided by 100'.

★ Why percentages?

Percentages are used in everyday life in all sorts of different ways. Look out for these ways, such as:

- Sale 50% off
- Bloggs Bank offers 5% interest on savings
- Smith: only 60% chance of playing in match

★ Word wise

Percent means 'out of 100'. **Per** means 'out of' and **cent** is 100, as in words like *centimetre, century*.

★ Simplest form

A **fraction** can be changed to its **simplest form** by dividing the top number (the numerator) and bottom number (the denominator) by the same number.

Clues and tips

When changing a fraction to its simplest form, always look to see what number will divide exactly into the top number (the numerator) and the bottom number (the denominator).

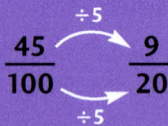

After dividing, check that there is not another whole number that will divide into both numbers. If there is not, the fraction is in its simplest form.

What next?

If you are fine with these, go on to page 7.

If not, read the tips above about how to change a fraction to its simplest form.

(You might also find the *Practise Fractions and decimals* book in this series useful.)

6

Try it yourself!

1 Approximately what percentage of each container is filled?

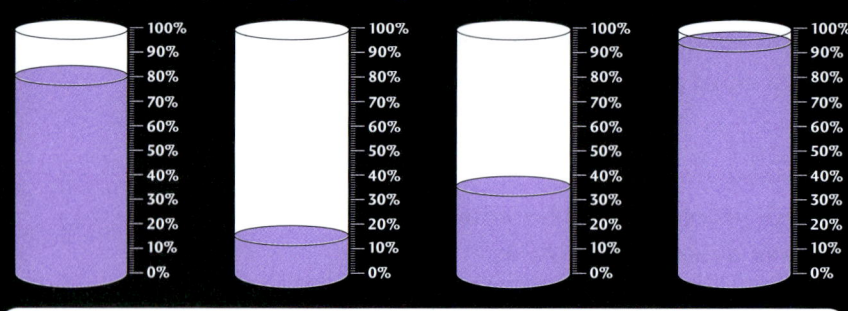

_____   _____   _____   _____

2 Write these percentages as fractions out of 100.

| 13% $\frac{13}{100}$ | 27% | 81% | 99% |
| 39% | 11% | 2% | 47% |

3 Write these percentages as division questions.

| 55% $55 \div 100$ | 38% _____ | 84% _____ |
| 13% _____ | 6% _____ | 10% _____ |

4 Write these percentages as fractions out of 100. Then change each fraction to its simplest form.

| 20% $\frac{20}{100} \xrightarrow{\div 20} \frac{1}{5}$ | 10% | 75% |
| 5% | 80% | 2% |

Have you got it?

Tick here

I know that the % sign means 'out of 100' or 'divided by 100'

I can write percentages as fractions (out of 100) and as division questions (divided by 100)

I can change a fraction to its simplest form

Percentages, fractions and decimals

Another language

- Percentages, fractions and decimals are like three different languages.

  They are just different ways of describing the same thing.

- Remember that percentages can be written as fractions and that some percentages can be written as *more than one* fraction, for example:

  50% can be written as $\frac{50}{100}$ or $\frac{1}{2}$

- Percentages can also be written as decimals. It is easy if the percentage is written as a division question.

  24% is 24 ÷ 100

  24 ÷ 100 = 0.24

  Work this division question out in your head or using a calculator to get a decimal answer.

Try it yourself!

Pick a percentage card and write it as a division question. Then work out the answer as a decimal in your head or using a calculator.

 42 ÷ 100 = 0.42

Look for a pattern as to what happens when you divide a number by 100. You will soon discover how easy it is.

Remember these rules:

Percentage
32%

Write the number out of 100 → Fraction: $\frac{32}{100}$

Divide the number by 100 → Decimal: 32 ÷ 100 = 0.32

If possible, change the fraction to its simplest form.

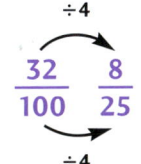

$\frac{32}{100}$ $\frac{8}{25}$ (÷4)

This has shown that:
$32\% = \frac{8}{25} = 0.32$

★ Percentages, fractions and decimals

Percentages, fractions and decimals are all used to describe what part of a whole something is.

If someone asked what proportion of a class was girls, the answer could be given as a fraction, e.g. $\frac{1}{2}$, as a percentage, e.g. 50%, or as a decimal, e.g. 0.5.

★ Dividing by 100

It is easy to divide by 100 in your head.

Just move the digits of the number two places to the right. The decimal point remains in the same place.

★ H T U . t h

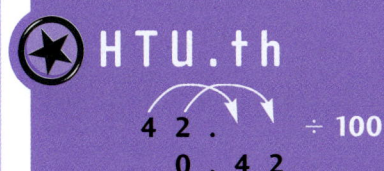

Notice that we write 0.42 rather than .42 as it is easy to miss the decimal point otherwise.

7

Clues and tips

If you are not sure about dividing by 100 in your head, use a calculator to divide each number by 100 first. Once you spot the pattern, keep going in your head.

Word wise

Convert is another word for 'change'.

Decimal details

The decimal 0.20 is the same as 0.2.

There is *no* need to write a zero at the right-hand end of a decimal.

0.50 = 0.5

0.30 = 0.3

What next?

If you are fine with these ideas, go on to page 9.

However, you might still find changing fractions to their simplest form difficult. Do not worry. As long as you can write them as fractions out of 100 at the moment, you will be okay to move on to page 9.

If you feel you still need more practice, use your percentage cards.

Try it yourself!

1 Divide each of these numbers by 100 in your head.

25 _0.25_   32 _____   67 _____   21 _____   86 _____
5 _____   3 _____   20 _____   50 _____   80 _____

2 **Convert** each percentage into a **decimal** in your head.

55% _55 ÷ 100 = 0.55_   35% _____   74% _____
18% _____   7% _____   32% _____
10% _____   99% _____   100% _____
1% _____   40% _____   33% _____

3 **Convert** each percentage into a **fraction** and **decimal**.

Percentage	Fraction (in its simplest form)	Decimal
30%	$\frac{30}{100} = \frac{3}{10}$	0.3
90%		
2%		
15%		
8%		

Have you got it?

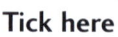 Tick here

I know that **percentages**, **fractions** and **decimals** can be used to describe parts of a whole

I can divide a number by 100 in my head

I can write percentages as **decimals** by dividing by 100

I can convert a percentage to a **fraction** and to a **decimal**

Calculating percentages in your head

Percentages of amounts

- There are many different ways to calculate a percentage of a number in your head.

Remember first that 50% is $\frac{1}{2}$, 25% is $\frac{1}{4}$ and 75% is $\frac{3}{4}$. Here are some of the ways:

- To calculate 50%: halve the number.

  50% of £300 → half of £300 = £150

  50% of 820 g → half of 820 g = 410 g

- To calculate 25%: halve the number and halve the answer (or just divide by 4).

  25% of £300 → half of £300 = £150 → half of £150 = £75

  25% of 820 g → half of 820 g = 410 g → half of 410 g = 205 g

- To calculate 75%: halve the number and halve the answer. Then add the two answers together.

  75% of £300 → half of £300 = £150 / half of £150 = £75
  → £150 + £75 = £225

  75% of 820 g → half of 820 g = 410 g / half of 410 g = 205 g
  → 410 g + 205 g = 615 g

Try it yourself!

You will need these three percentage cards 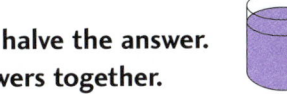 from page 15. Also cut out the number cards on page 17.

Pick a number card and a percentage card and calculate that percentage of the number in your head.

 of 120 = 60

Do this as many times as you can until you get the hang of it.

★ Word wise

Calculate does *not* mean 'use a calculator'.

It means 'work out the answer'.

You can calculate in your head, on paper or using a calculator.

★ Halving numbers

If the number is quite difficult to halve, it can be split into easier parts like this:

Half of 172

Split 172 into parts . . .

100 70 2

and halve each part.

50 35 1

Then add them back together again.

Half of 172 =

50 + 35 + 1 = 86

The number can be split in different ways:

Half of 172

Split 172 into parts . . .

160 12

and halve each part.

80 6

So

Half of 172 = 80 + 6 = 86

Clues and tips

If the number is quite difficult to halve, it can be split into easier parts.

Use a number line

If you find it difficult to keep track of numbers in your head, you might find this useful.

Draw a line like this:

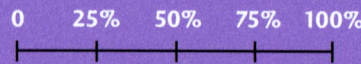

Write the amount underneath the 100%, like this:

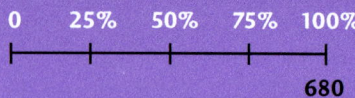

Then, as you work out 50% and 25%, etc., write them under the line.

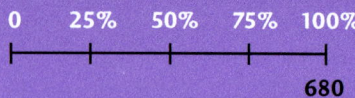

What next?

If you are fine with these, go on to page 11. If not, read the tips above again and practise more with the cut-out cards.

10

Try it yourself!

1 Calculate each of these percentages in your head.

50% of £600 _£300_	50% of £120 _____	50% of £680 _____
50% of 72 kg _____	50% of 48 kg _____	50% of 840 kg _____
25% of £600 _____	25% of £120 _____	25% of £680 _____
25% of 72 kg _____	25% of 48 kg _____	25% of 840 kg _____
75% of £600 _____	75% of £120 _____	75% of £680 _____
75% of 72 kg _____	75% of 48 kg _____	75% of 840 kg _____

2 Calculate each of these percentages in your head.

25% of £160 _____	50% of £110 _____	75% of £88 _____
50% of 70 kg _____	25% of 180 kg _____	50% of 290 kg _____
75% of 16 ml _____	75% of 140 ml _____	25% of 460 ml _____
25% of 144 m _____	75% of 36 m _____	50% of 184 m _____

3 Calculate each of the percentages to solve these problems.

In a sale you pay 75% of the ticket price. The ticket price for a coat is £56. How much is the sale price?

A man pays 25% of his earnings in tax. He earns £24 000 in a year. How much tax does he pay?

A mobile phone company has a 50% sale. How much will a phone cost in the sale if it usually costs £78?

Have you got it?

Tick here

I can **calculate** 50% of a number in my head by halving

I can **calculate** 25% of a number in my head by halving and halving again

I can **calculate** 75% of a number in my head by adding the answers to 50% and 25% together

Calculating other percentages

Divide by ten

- Other percentages can be found in your head by first finding 10%.

0	10%	20%	30%	40%	50%	60%	70%	80%	90%	100%
0	$\frac{1}{10}$	$\frac{2}{10}$	$\frac{3}{10}$	$\frac{4}{10}$	$\frac{1}{2}$	$\frac{6}{10}$	$\frac{7}{10}$	$\frac{8}{10}$	$\frac{9}{10}$	1

- To calculate 10%: divide the number by 10.
  10% of £300 → £300 ÷ 10 = £30
  10% of 820 g → 820 g ÷ 10 = 82 g

- To calculate 20%: divide by 10 and double.
  20% of £300 → £300 ÷ 10 = £30 → £30 × 2 = £60
  20% of 820 g → 820 g ÷ 10 = 82 g → 82 g × 2 = 164 g

- To calculate 30%: divide by 10 and multiply by 3.
  30% of £300 → £300 ÷ 10 = £30 → £30 × 3 = £90
  30% of 820 g → 820 g ÷ 10 = 82 g → 82 g × 3 = 246 g

- To calculate 40%: divide by 10 and multiply by 4.

> For *all percentages that are multiples of 10*, the answer to 10% can be used to calculate percentages of amounts.

Try it yourself!

You will need the percentage cards that show multiples of 10 and the number cards from page 17.

| 10% | 20% | 30% | 40% | 50% | 60% | 70% | 80% | 90% |

Pick a number card and a percentage card and calculate that percentage of the number in your head.

30% of 120 = 12 × 3 = 36

Do this as many times as you can until you get the hang of it.

Check that the answer is 'about right'.

30% is just a bit more than 25% or $\frac{1}{4}$.
$\frac{1}{4}$ of 120 = 30.   36 is a bit more than 30.
So it is about right.

Dividing by 10

Remember that when a number is divided by 10, the digits move one place to the right.

H T U . t h
1 4 0 . ÷ 10
  1 4 . 0

There is no need to write a zero at the right-hand end of a decimal.

14.0 = 14

50.0 = 50

A different way for 90%

When finding 90%, first find 10%. Rather than multiplying the answer by 9, it might be sometimes easier to subtract 10% from the original answer (100%), like this:

> Find 90% of 120.

10% of 120 = 12

Then, rather than calculating 12 × 9 to find 90%, subtract 12 from 120.

120 − 12 = 108

so 90% of 120 = 108

11

Clues and tips

Remember that when a number is **divided by 10**, the digits move one place to the right.

H T U . t h
  4 6 .   ÷ 10
     4 . 6

Use a number line

If you find it difficult to keep track of numbers in your head, you might find this useful.

Draw a line like this:

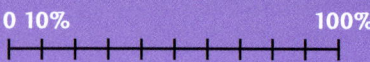

Write the amount underneath the 100% and 10%, like this:

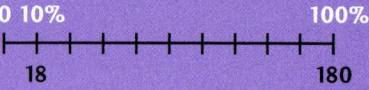

Then, as you work out 20% and 30%, etc., write them under the line.

What next?

If you are finding the multiplication part difficult, re-read the instructions above and try drawing the line to help you. Practise further with your cards if you need to.

Try it yourself!

1 Calculate each of these percentages in your head.

10% of £600 _£60_	10% of £120 ____	10% of £680 ____
10% of 72 kg _7.2 kg_	10% of 48 kg ____	10% of 84 kg ____
20% of £600 ____	20% of £120 ____	20% of £680 ____
20% of 72 kg ____	20% of 48 kg ____	20% of 84 kg ____

2 Calculate each of these percentages in your head.

30% of £60 ____	60% of £40 ____	80% of £90 ____
40% of 70 kg ____	90% of 110 kg ____	20% of 35 kg ____
70% of 80 ml ____	40% of 120 ml ____	80% of 300 ml ____
90% of 140 m ____	70% of 110 km ____	30% of 184 m ____

3 Calculate each of the percentages to solve these problems.

In a sale you pay 80% of the ticket price.
The ticket price for a coat is £60.
How much is the sale price?

A woman pays 30% of her earnings in tax.
She earns £12 000 in a year.
How much tax does she pay?

A baby girl weighs 90% of her expected weight.
Her expected weight was 130 ounces.
How much does she weigh?

Have you got it?

Tick here

I know how to find **10%** of a number by dividing by 10

I can **calculate** 20%, 30%, 40%, ..., 90% of a number, using my answer to 10% to help me

I can solve percentage problems in my head

Calculating percentages with a calculator

Percentage times

- Because a percentage can be written as a fraction or decimal, there are different ways of calculating percentages on a calculator.

As a fraction

Remember that a percentage can be written as a fraction 'out of 100' or 'divided by 100'.

To find 32% of £146 on a calculator, 32% can be keyed in as a fraction.

 $\frac{32}{100} \times £146 = £46.72$ ← Key into the calculator 32 ÷ 100 and then × 146

Notice that the multiplication key is used in place of the word 'of'.

As a decimal

Another way is to write each percentage as a decimal. Remind yourself how on page 7.

To find 32% of £146 on a calculator, 32% can be keyed in as a decimal.

 0.32 × £146 = £46.72

Choose which way you like best and remember to use the multiplication key in place of the word 'of'.

- Always remember to check your answer, whichever way you do it.

    32% of £146 = £46.72 →

    check
    32% is slightly less than one-third.
    $\frac{1}{3}$ of £150 = £50
    £46.72 is slightly less than £50.
    So it is about right.

★ A different way of looking at it

There are different ways of solving percentage questions.

Here is another method.

> Find 27% of 172.

First, find what 1% of this number is.

172 divided by 100

Then multiply to find what 27% is.

1.72 × 27

It does not matter which way this is done – the answer will be the same.

★ Check it

Check to get a rough idea of the size the answer should be. Always round the percentage and the number to make a rough calculation to see if the answer is about right.

Try it yourself! ▼

You will need all your percentage cards, the number cards from page 17 and a calculator.

| 10% | 2% | 15% | 3% | 53% | 99% | 18% | 28% |

Pick a number card and a percentage card, and calculate that percentage of the number on a calculator.

 53% of 120 = 63.6

Do this as many times as you can until you get the hang of it. Do not forget to check your answers.

13

Clues and tips

Change the percentage to a decimal and then just multiply.

Decimal difficulties

Watch out for answers appearing on the calculator that do not make sense. How much is £13.466839?

If you are talking about money, then round the answer to the nearest penny – £13.47.

What next?

Do you feel you understand the ideas in the book so far? Now is a good time to look back and go over the pages to check that you still understand.

For the next part of the book, you will need to be able to calculate percentages of any amounts with a calculator. If you need to, use your cards for more practice of this.

Try it yourself!

1 Calculate each of these percentages on a calculator.

32% of £60 _____	64% of £48 _____	88% of £97 _____
42% of 70 kg _____	18% of 112 kg _____	46% of 35 kg _____
17% of 87 ml _____	29% of 125 ml _____	82% of 305 ml _____
99% of 145 m _____	72% of 118 m _____	36% of 184 m _____

2 Solve these problems using a calculator.

In a sale you pay 84% of the ticket price. The ticket price for a coat is £24. How much is the sale price? _____

A man pays 28% of his earnings in tax. He earns £15 000 in a year. How much tax does he pay? _____

A baby girl weighs 86% of her expected weight. If her expected weight was 130 ounces, how much does she weigh? _____

A car is travelling at 54 mph. It slows down to travel at 67% of that speed. How fast is the car travelling now? _____

I have £365 in my bank account. I earn 3.5% interest on this money. How much interest do I earn? _____

A restaurant adds a 12% service charge to the cost of a meal. How much is the service charge for a meal costing £35? _____

Have you got it?

Tick here

I can write percentages as decimals by dividing by 100 ☐

I can calculate percentages of amounts on a calculator ☐

I can solve problems involving percentages ☐

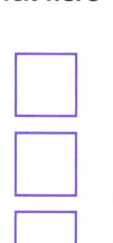

Activity cards

Percentage cards

20%	80%	5%	0%	41%	71%	99%
10%	70%	3%	15%	39%	67%	95%
75%	60%	2%	12%	32%	65%	100%
25%	40%	1%	11%	28%	53%	85%
50%	30%	90%	7%	23%	45%	72%

16

Number cards

200	140	180	660	360
80	760	580	420	320
40	800	340	480	280
120	160	260	220	240

Writing something as a percentage

Time for a change

- Up to now, almost every question in this book has had a percentage in it. Like these:

  Convert this percentage into a decimal: **55%**

  Calculate **32%** of £60.

  In a sale you pay **84%** of the ticket price.
  The ticket price for a coat is £24.
  How much is the sale price?

  For these types of questions, remember that the **%** sign means 'out of 100' or 'divided by 100'.

- The questions that follow do *not* have a percentage in them. In these questions the ANSWER is a percentage.

  Like this:

  Jo got **54** marks in a test out of a total of **60** marks. Give Jo's score as a **percentage**.

  → No percentage given

  ↑ Answer will be a percentage

- For this type of question:

  a) write a number as a **fraction** of another
  b) multiply by 100.   **(Yes, it is that easy.)**

  a) Jo got 54 out of 60. Write this as a **fraction**.
  b) Then multiply by 100.

  $$\frac{54}{60} \times 100$$

  Key into the calculator 54 ÷ 60 and then × 100

  Try this on a calculator. Do you get the answer 90%?
  Notice that your ANSWER is a percentage.

  Now try this one.

  Rob got 34 marks in a test out of a total of 40 marks.
  Give Rob's score as a percentage.

  $$\frac{34}{40} \times 100 = 85\%$$

  By changing both scores to percentages they can be compared to find out who scored the highest proportion of marks.

 Fraction line

When looking at a fraction, think of the **line** separating the two numbers as a **division** sign. When keying a fraction into a calculator, key in the top number (the numerator) and the divide sign, then the bottom number (the denominator). Like this:

$$\frac{1}{2} = 1 \div 2$$

$$\frac{3}{4} = 3 \div 4$$

 In your head

Without a calculator, change the fraction to its simplest form first (see page 6).

$$\frac{54}{60} \xrightarrow{\div 6} \frac{9}{10}$$
$$\xleftarrow{\div 6}$$

It is easier to multiply this by 100 in your head. Then, if possible, divide the denominator and 100 by the same number.

$$\frac{9}{10} \times 100 \quad \substack{\div 10 \\ \div 10}$$

$$= 9 \times 10 = 90\%$$

Clues and tips

When using a calculator, the answer might not be a whole number, e.g. 83.466839124.

Percentage answers should be rounded to one or two decimal places, e.g. **83.5%** or **83.47%**.

Without a calculator?

Remember to change each fraction to its simplest form first.

Then, if possible, divide the denominator and 100 by the same number, e.g. by 5.

What next?

If you are fine with these, go on to page 21.

If not, re-read the tips on page 6 about how to change a fraction to its simplest form.

(You might also find the *Practise Fractions and decimals* book in this series useful.)

20

Try it yourself!

1 Give the first number as a percentage of the second number. You can use a calculator. Round any decimals to 2 decimal places.

60 out of 75 $\frac{60}{75} \times 100 = 80\%$	51 out of 60 _____
48 out of 52 _____	11 out of 55 _____
58 out of 80 _____	112 out of 120 _____
45 out of 70 _____	40 out of 65 _____

2 Give each of these scores as a percentage. You can use a calculator. Round any decimals to 2 decimal places.

Who scored the highest percentage of marks?

Matt got 42 marks out of a total of 50 marks.

Richard got 64 marks out of a total of 70 marks.

Nicole got 73 marks out of a total of 80 marks.

Michelle got 33 marks out of a total of 40 marks.

Tom got 105 marks out of a total of 120 marks.

Jodie got 81 marks out of a total of 90 marks.

3 Answer these questions *without* using a calculator.

There were 150 people at a concert.
60 of the people were female.
What percentage were female?

There were 160 people at a funfair.
96 of the people were female.
What percentage were female?

Have you got it?

Tick here

I can give one number as a percentage of the other, **using a calculator**

I can solve questions where the answer is a percentage, **without a calculator**

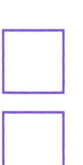

Problems, problems

Understanding what to do to solve a problem

- Most people find percentages difficult because percentage problems and puzzles always look very different from each other.

> 12% of a 150 g chocolate bar is nuts. How many grams of nuts are there?

> 24 out of every 300 people in the country wear contact lenses. What is this as a percentage?

> A bank paid Anna some interest on the £180 she had in the bank. It paid her £32. What is this as a percentage?

> A pack of biscuits usually has 20 biscuits. In a new pack, 15% more biscuits are included. How many extra biscuits is that?

When you see a problem, do not panic! Ask yourself these questions:

Has the question got a percentage in it?

Or *Am I supposed to give a percentage as an ANSWER?*

- If the question has a percentage in it, remember that the percentage sign means 'out of 100' or 'divided by 100'.

> 12% of a 150 g chocolate bar is nuts. How many grams of nuts are there?

12% of 150 g

$\frac{12}{100} \times 150\text{ g} = 18\text{ g}$

- If the ANSWER is to be a percentage, write the fraction and then multiply by 100.

> 24 out of every 300 people in the country wear contact lenses. What is this as a percentage?

$\frac{24}{300} \times 100 = 8\%$

Look carefully at every problem to work out which type it is. (Sometimes there might be an extra part to the question – these are looked at on the next few pages.)

★ Remember this

Do make sure that you read the question carefully to check you understand what it is asking for. Try to imagine the situation, drawing a small picture to help you, if you like.

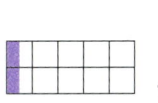

★ Forgotten how?

If you have forgotten how to answer both types of questions, look at page 13 for the first type and page 19 for the second type.

Divide by 100 if the question contains a percentage.

Multiply by 100 to get a percentage ANSWER.

(For the first type, the percentage could be changed to a decimal to key into a calculator – see page 13.)

Clues and tips

Remember to write the **unit or percentage sign** in the answer.

Interest and VAT

Money that is kept in a bank or building society account, is usually given 'interest'. Interest is some extra money that is given, calculated as a percentage of the money that is in the account.

VAT stands for 'Value Added Tax'. Shops charge VAT on most items that they sell.

VAT is usually charged at a rate of 17.5%.

What next?

If you are happy with solving these types of problems, go on to page 23. From page 23 onwards you will find out about questions that involve percentage increases and decreases.

22

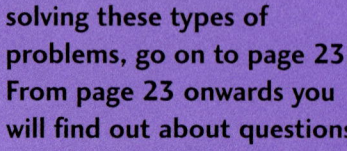

Try it yourself!

1 Solve these problems.

14% of a 250 g pot of yogurt is strawberries. How many grams of strawberries are there?

$\frac{14}{100} \times 250\,g = 35\,g$

16 out of every 250 people in the country wear glasses. What is this as a percentage?

A bank paid Anna some interest on the £180 she had in the bank. It paid her £32. What is this as a percentage?

A pack of biscuits usually has 20 biscuits. In a new pack, 15% more biscuits are included. How many extra biscuits is that?

A drink is made with 18% of the total liquid being blackcurrant juice. If 350 ml of drink is made, how much is blackcurrant juice?

In a phone bill, 17.5% VAT is added to the cost of calls. If the total cost of calls is £58, how much is VAT?

2 Solve these problems, reading the question carefully.

45% of the 120 pupils in Class 1W are boys. 65% of the 80 pupils in Class 2G are boys. Which class has most boys?

Megan scored 101 out of 130 in a test. Rachel scored 188 out of 220 in a test. Which girl had the higher percentage?

Have you got it?

Tick here

I can solve problems where percentages are given ☐

I can solve problems that have a percentage ANSWER ☐

I can tell which type of question is which ☐

Estimating percentage increases and decreases

Making things larger by increasing them

- When something is made larger, it is increased.
  Things can be increased *by a percentage*. Look at these examples:

Salaries are increased by 25%.

This packet is 25% larger than the standard packet.

A 1 month old baby now weighs 30% more than at birth.

This black line is increased by 50%.

The new line will have an extra 50% added on.

This black line is increased by 10%.

The new line will have an extra 10% added on.

This black line is increased by 100%.

The new line will have an extra 100% added on.

- When something is made smaller it is decreased.
  Things can be decreased *by a percentage*. Look at these examples:

Jim now weighs 40% less!

All prices reduced by 25%.

A 12% decrease in cases of measles last year.

This black line is decreased by 50%.

The new line will have 50% taken off.

This black line is decreased by 10%.

The new line will have 10% taken off.

This black line is decreased by 100%.

The new line will have 100% taken off.

Notice how the examples show a percentage *and* words like more, larger or increased by.

Notice that a 100% increase makes the new line double the length.

Notice how these examples show a percentage *and* words like less, reduced by or decreased by.

Notice that a 100% decrease leaves nothing.

Clues and tips

Notice that the starting lines are not always the same length.

This means that a **50%** increase for one length might be the *same actual size* as a **100%** increase for another length.

Always look at the *original length* before estimating the size of the increase.

Don't worry about estimating

People sometimes worry that their estimates will be wrong.

Here, estimating just gets you used to giving a rough idea of what percentage is added on.

What next?

If you feel that you understand what a percentage increase or decrease is, you are ready to solve problems with them. Go on to the next page. If not, practise some more with your cards.

Try it yourself!

1 **Estimate these percentage increases.**

This black line is **increased** by about ………% of its length.

50%

This black line is **increased** by about ………% of its length.

This black line is **increased** by about ………% of its length.

This black line is **increased** by about ………% of its length.

2 **Estimate these percentage decreases.**

This black line is **decreased** by about ………% of its length.

This black line is **decreased** by about ………% of its length.

This black line is **decreased** by about ………% of its length.

This black line is **decreased** by about ………% of its length.

Have you got it?

Tick here

I can estimate percentage **increases** and **decreases**

I know that a **100%** increase is **double** and that a **100%** decrease leaves you with **nothing**

Percentage increases

Find the percentage part and add it on

- Now that you understand what a percentage increase is, you can solve percentage increase problems.
- This is all you have to do:
  a) calculate the percentage of the amount given
  b) add it on.

- Here is an example:

  Increase £60 by 32%.   First find 32% of £60.

  £60

  $$\frac{32}{100} \times 60 = £19.20$$

  £60   £19.20

  Then add it on. → £60 + £19.20 = £79.20

- Here is another example:

  Increase £24 by 84%.   First find 84% of £24.

  £24

  $$\frac{84}{100} \times 24 = £20.16$$

  £24   £20.16

  Then add it on. → £24 + £20.16 = £44.16

- That is all there is to it, but sometimes the problems are worded in different ways. Try these.

  The number of biscuits in a packet has been increased by 15%. There used to be 20 biscuits in a packet. How many are there now?

  $$\frac{15}{100} \times 20 = 3$$

  $20 + 3 = 23$

  So now there are 23 biscuits altogether.

  There were 4700 people living in a village last year. This year the population has grown by 36%. How many people live in the village now?

  In a phone bill, VAT at 17.5% is added to the cost of calls. The cost of calls is £48. How much will the bill be, including VAT?

You can do this already

The first step is easy – you can already do this. See page 13 to remind yourself how.

Use a calculator.

Remember that the percentage sign means 'out of 100' or 'divided by 100', so key in

32 ÷ 100

and then use the × key in place of the word 'of'.

Alternatively, you might prefer to key in the decimal 0.32 before multiplying by 60.

The answer will be the same whichever way you do it.

Watch out for words that show an increase, like 'grow', 'more', 'increases', 'added', 'extra', 'larger'.

Clues and tips
Look back at page 13 for a reminder on how to find 64% of £25.

Watch out
Be careful when it comes to adding on.

Make sure that you add the original amount and not the percentage.

Checking
Check to get a rough idea of the size that your answer should be. Always round the percentage and the number to make a rough calculation to see if your answer is about right.

What next?
Hopefully, you are finding it relatively easy to do. If you are, then you will find the percentage decrease questions on the next page just as easy. If you are still stuck, then you may need to practise finding percentages of amounts again. Follow the Try it yourself! activity on page 13 again.

Try it yourself!

1 **Increase** each price by the percentage shown.

Increase £80 by 24% _____   Increase £25 by 64% _____

Increase £48 by 82% _____   Increase £93 by 13% _____

Increase £134 by 47% _____   Increase £228 by 73% _____

Remember to check your answers by making a rough approximation.

2 Solve these **percentage increase** problems.

A car is travelling at a 58 mph. The driver increases the car's speed by 18%. What is the car's new speed?   _____

Last year a man's mass was 58 kg. This year his mass has increased by 12%. What is the man's mass now?   _____

The population of a village has grown by 35% from 1560 people ten years ago. What is the population of the village now?   _____

In a phone bill, VAT at 17.5% is added to the total cost of calls. The total cost of calls is £68. How much will the bill be including VAT?   _____

Remember to check your answers by making a rough approximation.

Have you got it?

Tick here

I can **increase** a price by a percentage

I can solve **percentage increase** questions

I can check my answers by making a rough approximation

Percentage decreases

Find the percentage part and subtract it

- Now that you can solve **percentage increase** problems, you will find **percentage decrease** problems just as easy.
- This is all you have to do:
  a) **calculate** the percentage of the amount given
  b) **subtract** it.
- Here is an example:

Decrease £60 by 32%. First find 32% of £60.

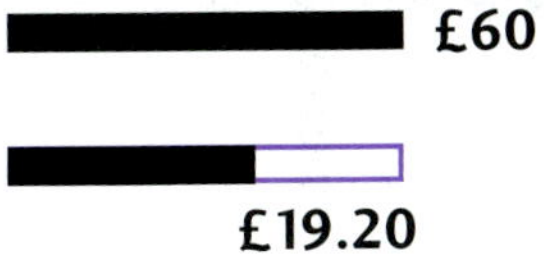

£60

£19.20

$$\frac{32}{100} \times 60 = £19.20$$

Then subtract it. → £60 − £19.20 = £40.80

- Here is another example:

Decrease £24 by 84%. First find 84% of £24.

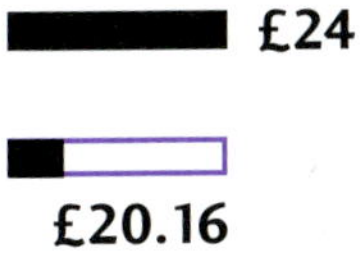

£24

£20.16

$$\frac{84}{100} \times 24 = £20.16$$

Then subtract it. → £24 − £20.16 = £3.84

- That is all there is to it, but sometimes the problems are worded in different ways. Try these.

The number of biscuits in a packet has been **decreased by 15%**. There used to be **20** biscuits in a packet. How many are there now?

$$\frac{15}{100} \times 20 = 3$$

$$20 - 3 = 17$$

So now there are 17 biscuits altogether.

There were **4789** people living in a village last year. This year the population has **reduced by 36%**. How many people live in the village now?

A shop offers a **65% discount** on all ticket prices. A jacket's ticket price is **£28**. How much will the jacket cost in the sale?

★ You can do this already

The first step is easy – you can already do this. See page 13 to remind yourself how.

Use a calculator.

Remember that the percentage sign means 'out of 100' or 'divided by 100' so key in

32 ÷ 100

and then use the × key in place of the word 'of'.

Alternatively, you might prefer to key in the **decimal** 0.32 before multiplying by 60.

The answer will be the same whichever way you do it.

Watch out for words that show a decrease, like 'less', 'off', 'decreased by', 'reduced', 'left', 'discount'.

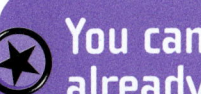

Clues and tips

Be careful when it comes to adding on.

Make sure that you subtract from the original amount and not from the percentage.

Learn to look

When faced with a percentage problem, learn to look for words that indicate that it is a percentage decrease question, like 'decrease', 'discount', 'fallen', 'reduced'.

What next?

Hopefully, you are finding it relatively easy to do. If you are, then you will find the questions on the next page just as easy. If you are stuck, then you may need to practise finding percentages of amounts again. Follow the **Try it yourself!** activity on page 13 again.

Try it yourself!

1 **Decrease** each price by the percentage shown.

Decrease £80 by 24% _____   Decrease £25 by 64% _____

Decrease £48 by 82% _____   Decrease £93 by 13% _____

Decrease £134 by 47% _____   Decrease £228 by 73% _____

Remember to check your answers by making a rough approximation.

2 Solve these **percentage decrease** problems.

A car is travelling at a 58 mph. The driver decreases the car's speed by 18%. What is the car's new speed?

Last year a man's mass was 58 kg. This year his mass has fallen by 12%. What is the man's mass now?

The population of a village has dropped by 35% from 1560 people ten years ago. What is the population of the village now?

A person pays 22% of his earnings in tax. He earns £28 000 each year. How much money will he have left after he has paid tax?

Remember to check your answers by making a rough approximation.

Have you got it?

Tick here

I can decrease a price by a percentage

I can solve percentage decrease questions

I can check my answers by making a rough approximation

Increasing and decreasing more than once

Real situations

- **Percentage increases** and **decreases** occur in many situations in **real life**. Look at these examples:

> When a person puts money into a savings account, they receive an extra percentage of that money called **interest**.

> In January, a shop reduces its prices for the sale. Those items not sold by February are reduced by a further percentage.

- In both examples, a percentage increase or decrease occurs *more than once*.

> Emily has £3000 in a bank. She receives 5% interest each year.
> **After Year 1:**
>   she receives 5% of £3000 (= £150), which is added to her money.
> **After Year 2:**
>   she receives 5% of £3150 (= £157.50), which is then added.

Notice that the first increase of 5% (£150) is *not the same amount* as the second increase of 5% (£157.50).

> A dress cost £200 in December. In January it is reduced by 15%. In February it is reduced by a further 15%.
> **January:**
>   The cost is reduced from £200 by 15% (£30 reduction).
> **February:**
>   The cost is reduced from £170 by 15% (£25.50 reduction).

Notice that the first decrease of 15% (£30) is *not the same amount* as the second decrease of 15% (£25.50).

- People often make the mistake of thinking that a percentage increase or decrease will be the same as the one that follows it.

- Is an increase of 10% followed by a further increase of 10% *the same* as an increase of 20%? Look at this example:

| Increase £300 by 10% | 10% of £300 = £30, £300 + £30 = £330 |

then

| Increase £330 by 10% | 10% of £330 is £33, £330 + £33 = £363 |

Is this the same as . . . ?

| Increase £300 by 20% | 20% of £330 is £60, £330 + £60 = £360 |
| | The answer is NO. They are *not* the same. |

 ## Interest

Money kept in a bank or building society account, is usually given **interest**.

Interest is some extra money that is given, calculated as a percentage of the money that is in the account.

 ## Don't be fooled

Imagine that there was a choice between two bank accounts.

One paid **8% interest each year for 2 years**, and another paid out **16% interest after 2 years**. Would both accounts give the same amount of interest after 2 years?

This is £3 more than this.

More confident with percentages now?

Tick the following topics you feel confident with:

Part 1
Estimating percentages (pages 3–4) ☐

Writing percentages as fractions out of 100 and in their simplest form (pages 5–6) ☐

Writing percentages as fractions and decimals (pages 7–8) ☐

Calculating percentages in your head (pages 9–12) ☐

Calculating percentages with a calculator (pages 13–14) ☐

Part 2
Writing one number as a percentage of another (pages 19–20) ☐

Solving percentage problems (pages 21–22) ☐

Estimating percentage increases and decreases (pages 23–24) ☐

Calculating percentage increases and decreases (pages 25–28) ☐

Increasing and decreasing more than once (pages 29–30) ☐

Read through any pages again to make sure that you understand.

Why not look at other books in this series to help you with areas you still might be unsure about?

Try it yourself!

1 Which is more and by how much?

| £2000 increased by 15%, followed by a further increase of 15% | OR | £2000 increased by 30%? |

15% of £2000 = £300
15% of £2300 = £345
Now worth £2645 ← *More by £45*   *30% of £2000 = £600*
Now worth £2600

| £5000 increased by 35%, followed by a further increase of 35% | OR | £5000 increased by 70%? |

| £4000 decreased by 30%, followed by a further decrease of 30% | OR | £4000 decreased by 60%? |

| £9000 decreased by 15%, followed by a further decrease of 15% | OR | £9000 decreased by 30%? |

Have you got it?

Tick here

I understand that one percentage increase or decrease will NOT be the same as one that follows it ☐

I know that an increase of 10% followed by a further increase of 10% is NOT the same as an increase of 20% ☐

I know that a decrease of 10% followed by a further decrease of 10% is NOT the same as a decrease of 20% ☐